Fact Finders®

TechSafetySmarts

Cell Phone Safety

by Kathy Allen

Consultant:
Frank W. Baker
Media Literacy Consultant
Media Literacy Clearinghouse Inc.

CAPSTONE PRESS
a capstone imprint

Fact Finders are published by Capstone Press,
1710 Roe Crest Drive, North Mankato, Minnesota 56003
www.capstonepub.com

Library of Congress Cataloging-in-Publication Data
Allen, Kathy.
  Cell phone safety / by Kathy Allen.
     p. cm.—(Fact finders. Tech safety smarts)
  Includes bibliographical references and index.
  Summary: "Describes safe cell phone usage and ways to avoid dangerous
situations, such as identity theft, cyberbullying, or predators"—Provided by
publisher.
  ISBN 978-1-4296-9945-7 (library binding) — ISBN 978-1-62065-796-6 (pbk.)
  ISBN 978-1-4765-1572-4 (eBook PDF)
  1. Technology and children—Juvenile literature. 2. Cell phones—Security
measures—Juvenile literature. I. Title.
  HQ784.T37A45 2013
  395.5'9—dc23   2012020252

Editorial Credits
Jennifer Besel, editor; Sarah Bennett, designer; Laura Manthe, production specialist

Photo Credits
Capstone Studio: Karon Dubke, 20; Dreamstime: Aprescindere, 21 (inset), Mikael
Damkier, 21 (top); iStockphotos: sturti, 29; Shutterstock: Black Rock Digital, 25,
Christos Georghiou, 5, Christy Thompson, 23 (kids), Cienpies Design, 7, cobalt88, 14
(phone), ColinCramm, 14 (inset), Curioso, 10 (top), gezzeg, 4, gst, 12 (phone), Helder
Almeida, 17, Irina_QQQ, 12 (background), 14-15 (background), Ivonne Wierink, 9,
karen roach, 6, Kraska, 22, Merydolla, 23 (background), mistery, 1, Neo Edmund, 8,
Novelo, 12 (figures), pashabo, 27, planet5D LLC, 11, ponsuwan, 18, 19 (green signs),
Poulsons Photography, 11 (inset), SCOTTCHAN, 19 (yellow signs), vectorlib-com, 10
(bottom), Vereshchagin Dmitry, 18-19 (road), VLADGRIN, 28 (icons), VLADGRIN,
cover (phone, icons), YanLev, 26

Artistic Effects
Shutterstock: Bennyart, Eliks, JohnT Takai, nrt, Reno Martin, SoooInce,VLADGRIN

Printed in the United States of America in Stevens Point, Wisconsin.
022015   008778R

Table of Contents

Your Wired Life

You're working on your homework when you hear a familiar *bing*. It's your cell phone, alerting you to a new text message. Getting a text is nothing new but the number is. The text isn't from a friend in your contacts list. The message says, "Hey, what's up? What are you doing tonight?" You hit reply but before typing you think twice. Should you respond if you don't know who you're writing to?

If your parents or guardians have trusted you with a cell phone, it is likely a tool you use more than any other. You use it to talk to friends or call for a ride. Maybe you use it to go online for music and games or to post to social networking sites. A cell phone is a valuable tool that lets you stay in touch with friends and family—anytime, anywhere. But having a cell phone also comes with a big responsibility.

Throughout this book, you'll find "Talk about It" boxes that set up real-life situations you might run into. Use these boxes as discussion starters at home or at school. Talk about the pros and cons of different actions, and decide how you could stay safe in each situation.

So, should you respond to a text from an unknown number?

Only You Have the Power

Cell phones are so much fun, it's easy to forget they're not toys. But your parents or guardians expect you to use your phone in a mature way. What does that mean? For starters, it means to follow the rules. If your parents tell you the phone is just for calls, don't text or go online. Your school also has cell phone rules. If the rule says to turn phones off during the day, do it.

It's tempting to break the rules, especially if all your friends do. But gaining your parents' or guardians' trust will mean more freedom in the long run.

NO TEXTING ZONE

You're in charge of your own safety when you use a cell phone too. What about the text from an unknown number? If a stranger had asked you the same question on the street, would you answer? No way! So you shouldn't answer on the phone either. Your wired life—on a computer or on a cell phone—is your real life. Only you have the power to make your cell phone a tool that is useful, fun, and safe.

◀ **Text Message** ▶

Hey! What are you doing tonight? Let's meet up.

4:16PM Today
From: 555-345-2189

All the Info

Posting on websites, playing online games, texting, and, of course, talking. It's amazing what you can do with your cell phone. But with every tap of your finger, you need to be aware of the information you're sending out.

There are two kinds of information—private and public. What's the difference? Public information helps others get to know you. Telling people about your favorite food or pet lets them know what you like. But private information is just what the name says. It's info that belongs only to you. Your name and **Social Security number** are examples of private info.

TaLK about it

You're playing an online game with a stranger over your phone. You get this message from your game partner: Good game! How old are you?

What do you do?

SOCIAL SECURITY

123-4567-890

This Number Has Been Established For

Social Security number—an identification number that is assigned to only you

Sharing private information in texts or online is dangerous. You wouldn't give a stranger at the mall your address. Giving out your address in a text is just as risky. Just because it's on a screen doesn't make the action any different.

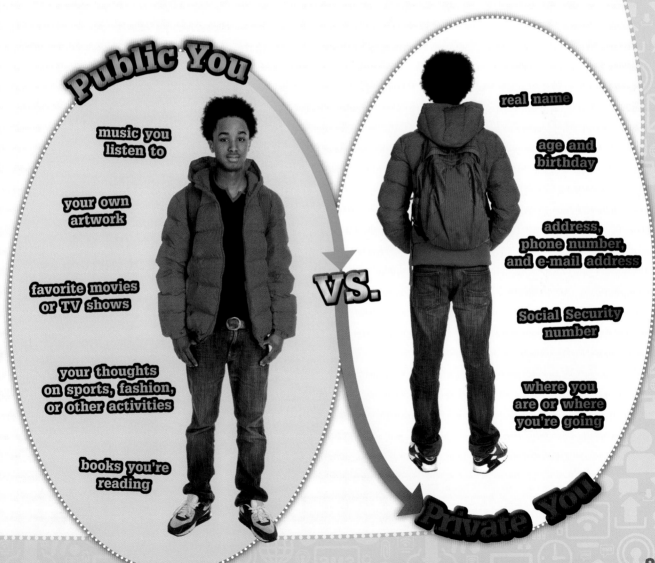

Public You

music you listen to

your own artwork

favorite movies or TV shows

your thoughts on sports, fashion, or other activities

books you're reading

VS.

real name

age and birthday

address, phone number, and e-mail address

Social Security number

where you are or where you're going

Private You

What's the Harm?

It makes sense not to give someone your address. But what could happen if you share other kinds of personal information? One possible problem is **identity** theft. This kind of theft happens when someone else uses your personal information.

If thieves get your Social Security number, they could apply for credit cards or **loans** while pretending to be you! When it's time to pay back the debt, identity thieves are nowhere to be found. Then when you need a car loan or a new phone, banks and stores might turn you down.

identity—who you are

loan—money borrowed from a bank

Erika Robbins
Today at 6:00pm

Headed to the homecoming game tonight! Can't wait!!!

Like - Comment   👍11 💬6

Another reason to keep personal information private is so dangerous people can't find you. Even where you are or where you're going should be private. A quick post from your phone, telling your friends you're headed to the game might seem harmless. But there's always a possibility that a criminal could see that post and head to the game too. And if a stranger texts you asking where you are, don't respond. Tell a trusted adult about the message, and then delete it.

TaLK about it

You get a text from an unknown number. It says you've won $1,500 to spend at your favorite store. You just have to respond with your name, birthday, and address.

What do you do?

Cyberbullying

Chatting and texting with friends are big parts of what make a cell phone fun. But nothing kills the fun like a bully. Cyberbullies use cell phones or computers to bully other people. Cyberbullying comes in many forms. If someone continues to tease you, shares your private info, or pretends to be you—that's cyberbullying.

Embarrassing a person is not OK—online or off. If you've ever gotten a mean text or phone call, you know how much it can hurt. And without seeing the hurt they cause, bullies are often even meaner behind the screen.

In the NEWS

Georgia was 13 years old when she started getting mean texts from other girls at school. Girls who were once her friends started calling her fat and ugly. It was as if the bullies were in her own home. Nowhere was safe. But Georgia did a smart thing. She shared what was happening with her mom. Her mom and other people helped her deal with the bullying. To help others with the same problem, Georgia became a mentor in an anti-bullying program at school.

Georgia's last name is left out to protect her privacy.

It's Not Your Fault

If someone is bullying you by phone, you need to know that it is not your fault. Cyberbullies are people who have low **self-esteem**. They are usually dealing with problems, such as a rough home life. Or maybe they are the victims of bullying too. They try to control other people to feel better about themselves.

self-esteem—a feeling of pride and respect for oneself

But you can take back control. Don't respond to a mean or threatening text. Instead, show the message to a parent or trusted adult. It might take some courage, but telling adults is very important. They can help you block unwanted calls from your phone. They can also decide if other parents or your school should get involved.

In the news

Josh had been bullied from the time he was 8 years old. When he was 15, that bullying became cyberbullying. He got several mean texts each day from a number he didn't know. He didn't want to tell his parents because he was embarrassed. But he says the bullying ended once he finally told someone. "Anyone being bullied needs to tell their parents or teacher because otherwise it will just keep going," he says.

Josh's last name is left out to protect his privacy.

Are You the Bully?

You might know one or two kids at school who could be called bullies. But have you ever thought of yourself as a cyberbully? It's easy to send a text or an e-mail when you're mad. Insulting someone is a lot easier "behind the screen." But remember that words—even words on a phone—hurt.

You can also become a cyberbully without meaning to. Forwarding hurtful texts or e-mails is cyberbullying. You may not have written the message. But if you send it, you've become part of the problem.

Being a cyberbully has **consequences**. Your parents could end up taking away your phone. Even worse, your actions could cost you your friendships. Before you send, stop and think about your message. How would you feel if your text was printed in the newspaper right under your photo and name? If you aren't proud of what you're sending, don't send it.

Talk about it

You get a text from a friend who says he's mad at your other friend. He calls the other friend names and even threatens to start a fist fight.

What do you do?

consequence—the result of an action

Stop, Drop, and Roll

This phrase isn't just for fire safety anymore. Remember to do it when you're on a cell phone too. Stop typing that message. Drop your phone for a bit. And roll these questions around in your head:

Should I say it that way?
Swear words and insults never make a situation better.

Why am I sending this message?
Before hitting send, be honest with yourself. Decide if you're truly trying to resolve a conflict or if you're secretly trying to get a little payback.

Who is the message going to?
Some messages are personal and should only go to one specific friend, instead of the whole gang.

Would I say that to the person's face?
If you wouldn't say or do it in front of the person, don't do it on the phone either.

Owning Your Safety

Having a cell phone is a big responsibility. Ultimately, you're the one in charge of your own safety when you use it. Watching out for trouble is kind of like crossing the street. On the road, you use crosswalks and traffic lights. You also look both ways for oncoming cars. On a phone, there aren't crosswalks, but there are things you can do to stop oncoming danger.

Never download ring tones or respond to texts about contests without asking your parents or guardians first. Even a simple online survey can be a **scam** to gather your private information.

Use **software** to block inappropriate websites on your phone. That way you don't accidently end up somewhere you don't want to be.

If you use your phone to chat online, use sites that have monitors. Monitors are people on the site who can help if you feel another user is being inappropriate.

scam—a false or untrustworthy act

software—the programs that tell the hardware of a computer what to do

Missing!

Pretend that one day you reach for your phone, but it's not there. It's not in your backpack or in your room. It's not in the car or under the couch. Your phone is lost or maybe even stolen!

Losing a phone really stinks. But losing your phone could be more than inconvenient. If someone finds it and starts snooping around, what might he or she learn? Think about what's in your e-mails or texts. Do they share any private information? Take it one step further. Someone could use the phone to send messages while posing as you.

Panthers W
Try Ou

5:00 this Thur.

Sign up for time
Coach Guenther'

*Bring your permissio

Don't freak out, though. There are some things you can do now to protect yourself. Your phone should allow you to lock the keypad with a password. Set up a password that no one could guess. Also, just say "no" when sites ask to remember your login and password. These small actions could make a big difference if your phone goes missing.

Online Forever

Using a password is a smart way to keep private info on your phone safe. But once info leaves your phone, it's not private anymore. Always keep in mind that what you post online is never private. Every time you share a text, picture, status update, e-mail, or video, it no longer belongs to you. What you share online is forever. Even postings on a site that is no longer active can still be found in Internet searches. **Stop, drop, and roll** before you post anything.

Before posting, check your privacy settings too. Some sites can track your location. Turn features like this off. Where you are or where you are going is personal information. It should never be shared on the Internet. Turning this setting off helps prevent dangerous people online from finding you offline.

12:45

John's phone is here.

Stop, Drop, and Roll

Avoid Embarrassment

Even if you follow all the rules, you might run into a conversation on the phone that makes you uncomfortable. Flirting in texts or sending inappropriate pictures may seem harmless. But texts that you thought were private can easily be shared with others. Messages or pictures sent in fun could turn embarrassing.

Protect yourself, and don't send inappropriate messages. And if you receive messages that make you uncomfortable, tell your parents or other trusted adults right away.

Parents and Trusted Adults

There are a lot of things you can do to keep yourself safe. But sometimes situations come up that you can't control. Don't hesitate to talk to your parents or other trusted adults about anything that happens when you're on your phone.

Talk about it

Your friend texts you a link to a video. You click on it and end up at an inappropriate website.

What do you do?

Talking to adults isn't always easy. It can be embarrassing or even a little scary to tell them about what's going on. But know that they care about you. They want to help you stay safe. So talk to them! They may have ideas on handling the situation that you didn't think of.

Sucked In

Finally, beware of "screen sucking"—spending every waking hour staring at your phone. If you're glued to the screen, you're probably missing a lot of cool stuff happening off screen. Put your phone in its place. You likely do your homework, watch TV, and text, all at the same time. But try doing just one thing at a time. You might be surprised how much you enjoy not being distracted. If you are walking outside, it's especially important to put the phone away to watch for cars, bicyclists, and curbs!

Trust your feelings. If something feels weird, creepy, or uncomfortable, tell an adult.

Remember that what you text or post online from your phone is out there forever. There's no getting it back after you hit "send."

If you wouldn't do something in real life, don't do it over your phone.

CeLL Phone Safety Rules of Thumb

If you are talking about personal information, do it face-to-face.

Don't download ring tones, take online surveys, or vote with your phone, unless you have permission from a parent or guardian.

You Can Do It!

Following the cell phone safety rules will help keep you safe and keep your phone enjoyable.

Remember—what you do on your phone is real life. There are some dangers. But there's no need to turn it off forever. Be aware of what you're doing on your phone. And stay the same awesome person you are face-to-face. You'll find that using your phone has never been more fun.

Glossary

consequence (KAHN-suh-kwens)—the result of an action

identity (eye-DEN-ti-tee)—who you are

loan (LOHN)—money borrowed from a bank

scam (SKAM)—a false or untrustworthy act

self-esteem (SELF-ess-TEEM)—a feeling of pride and respect for oneself

Social Security number (SOH-shul si-KYOOR-i-tee NUHM-bur)—an identification number that is assigned to only you; it is used to receive government benefits and is needed in order to get jobs, loans, or credit cards

software (SAWFT-wair)—the programs that tell the hardware of a computer what to do

Read More

Botzakis, Stergios. *Entertainment and Gaming.* Mastering Media. Chicago: Raintree, 2011.

Higgins, Nadia. *How Cell Phones Work.* Mankato, Minn.: Child's World, 2012.

Schwartz, Heather E. *Cyberbullying.* Tech Safety Smarts. North Mankato, Minn.: Capstone Press, 2013.

Internet Sites

FactHound offers a safe, fun way to find Internet sites related to this book. All of the sites on FactHound have been researched by our staff.

Here's all you do:

Visit *www.facthound.com*

Type in this code: 9781429699457

Index